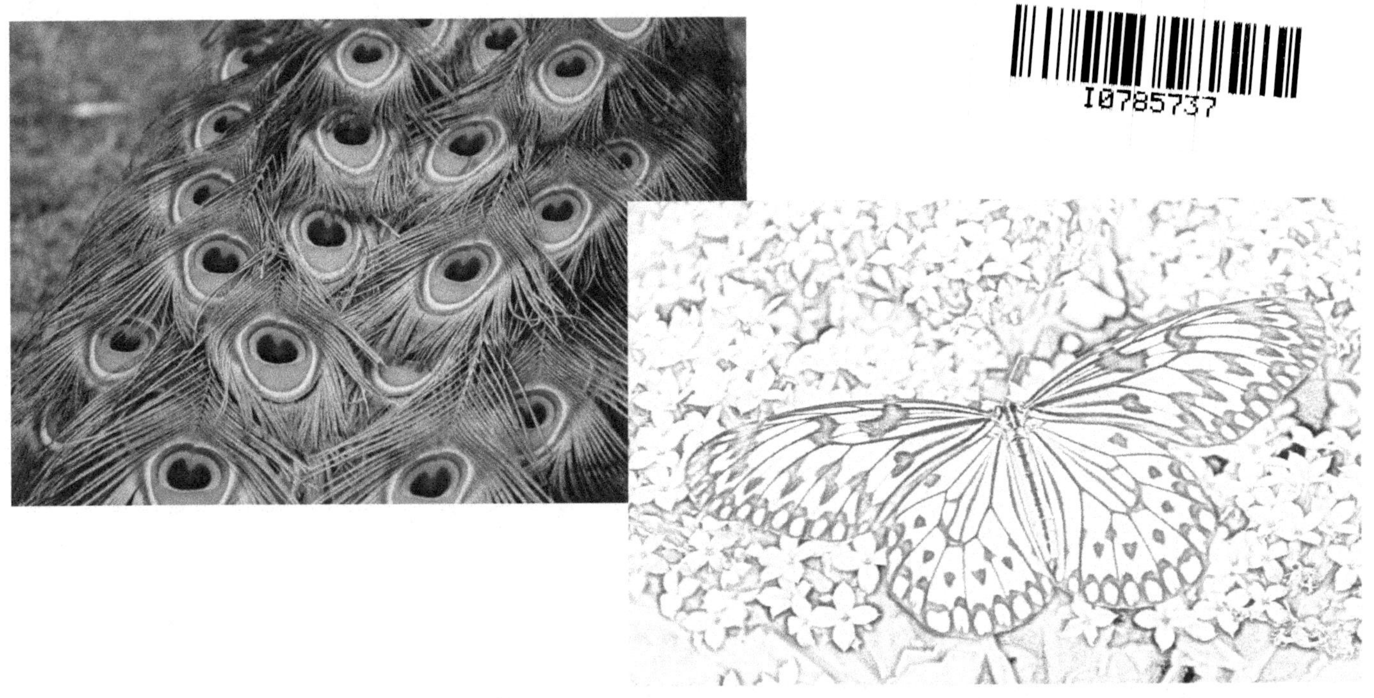

Relax, calm down and find inspiration in the semblance of peacocks and butterflies patterns. This coloring book contains 20 mixed images of different displays of peacocks and butterflies. It is made not to bore you out.

ISBN-13: 978-1722286231

ISBN-10: 1722286237

PEACOCKS AND BUTTERFLIES

Coloring Book for Adults

Illustrated

By

Wale Adio

1. Enchanting Display of a Peacock

2. Magical Display of Butterflies

3. The Crown and the King!

4. Can only be Created by the Mighty King!

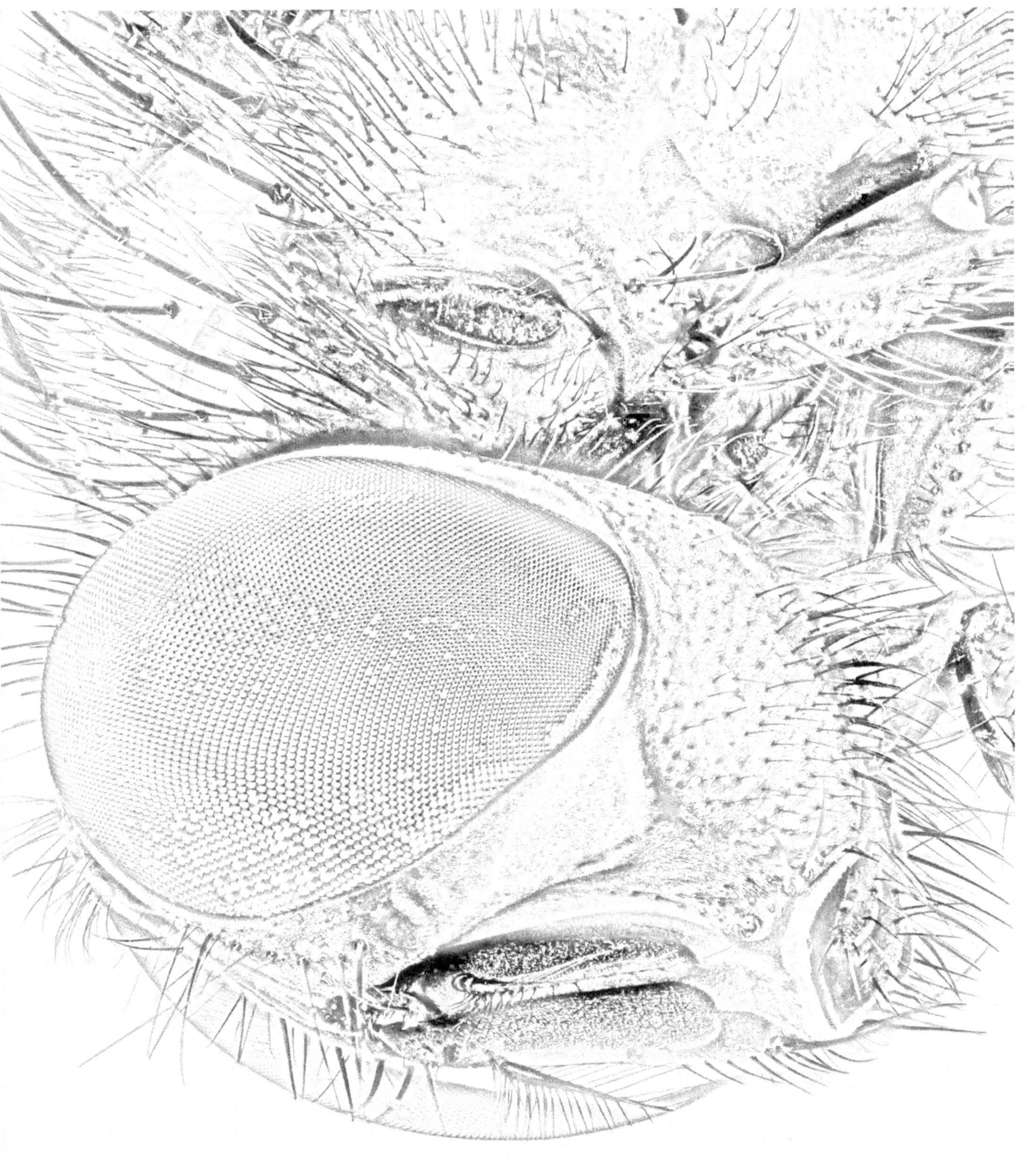

5. Complexity in a Simple Pattern

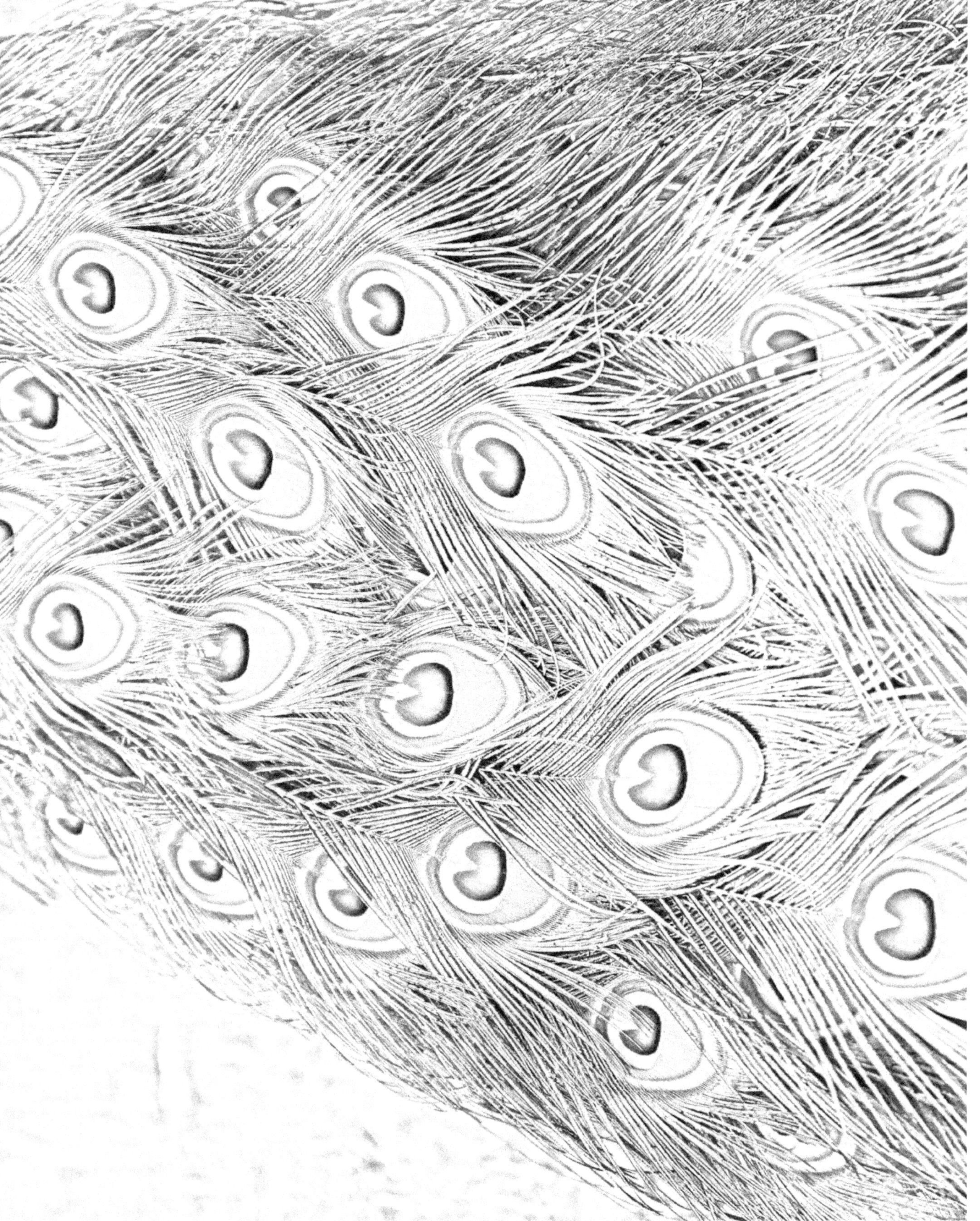

6. The Blossom of Spring

7. Book a Calming Session

8. Nature Rules!

9. Peacock and Peafowl

10.   Fly Butterfly!

11.   Beauty from the Back

12.   A Flying Pattern

13.   Caged!

14.   Nectar !

15.   Fictional Peacock Pattern

16.   Butterfly Paisley

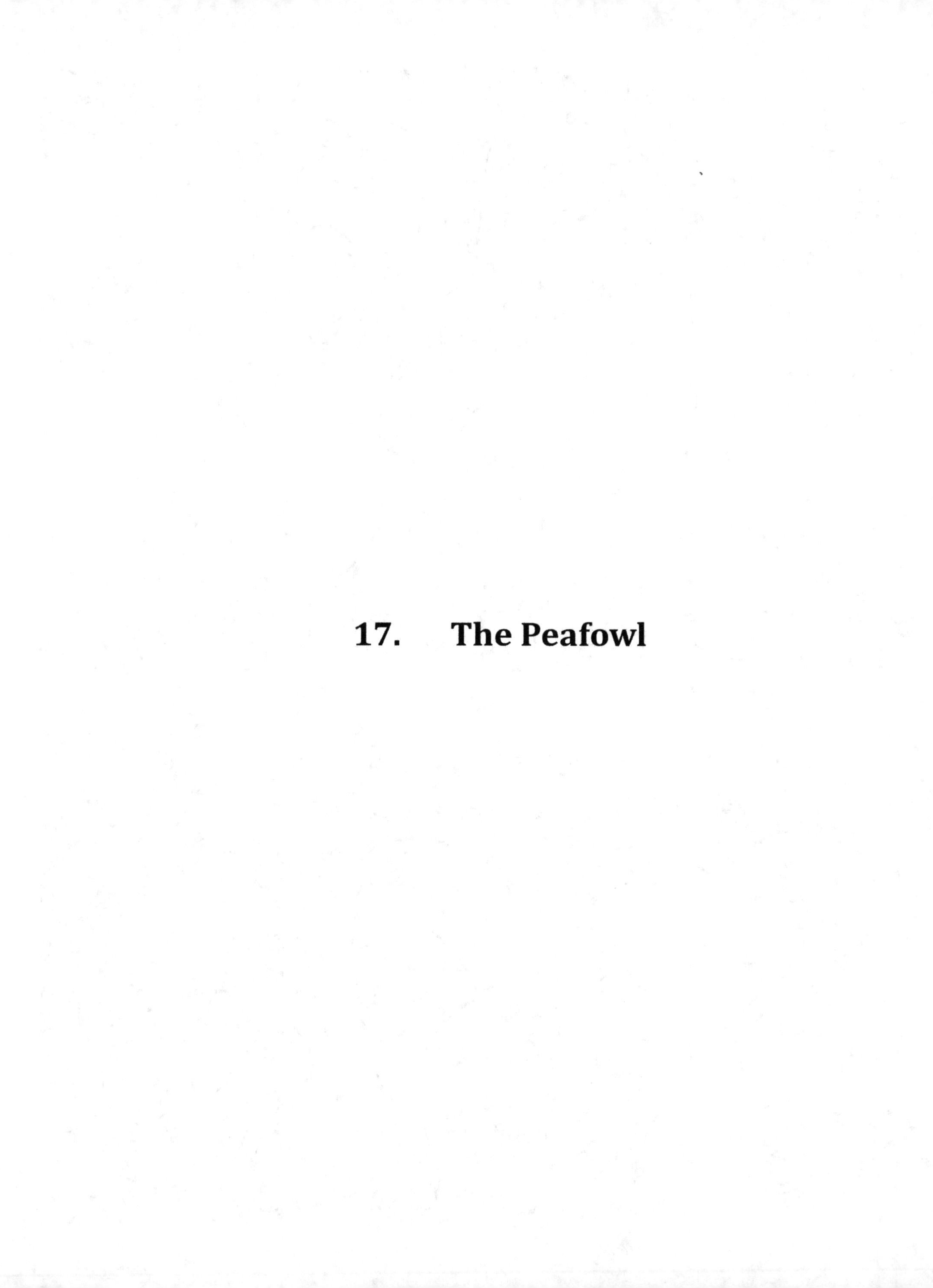

# 17.	The Peafowl

18.   Relax and Unlock your Imagination

19.　　The Peacock Family

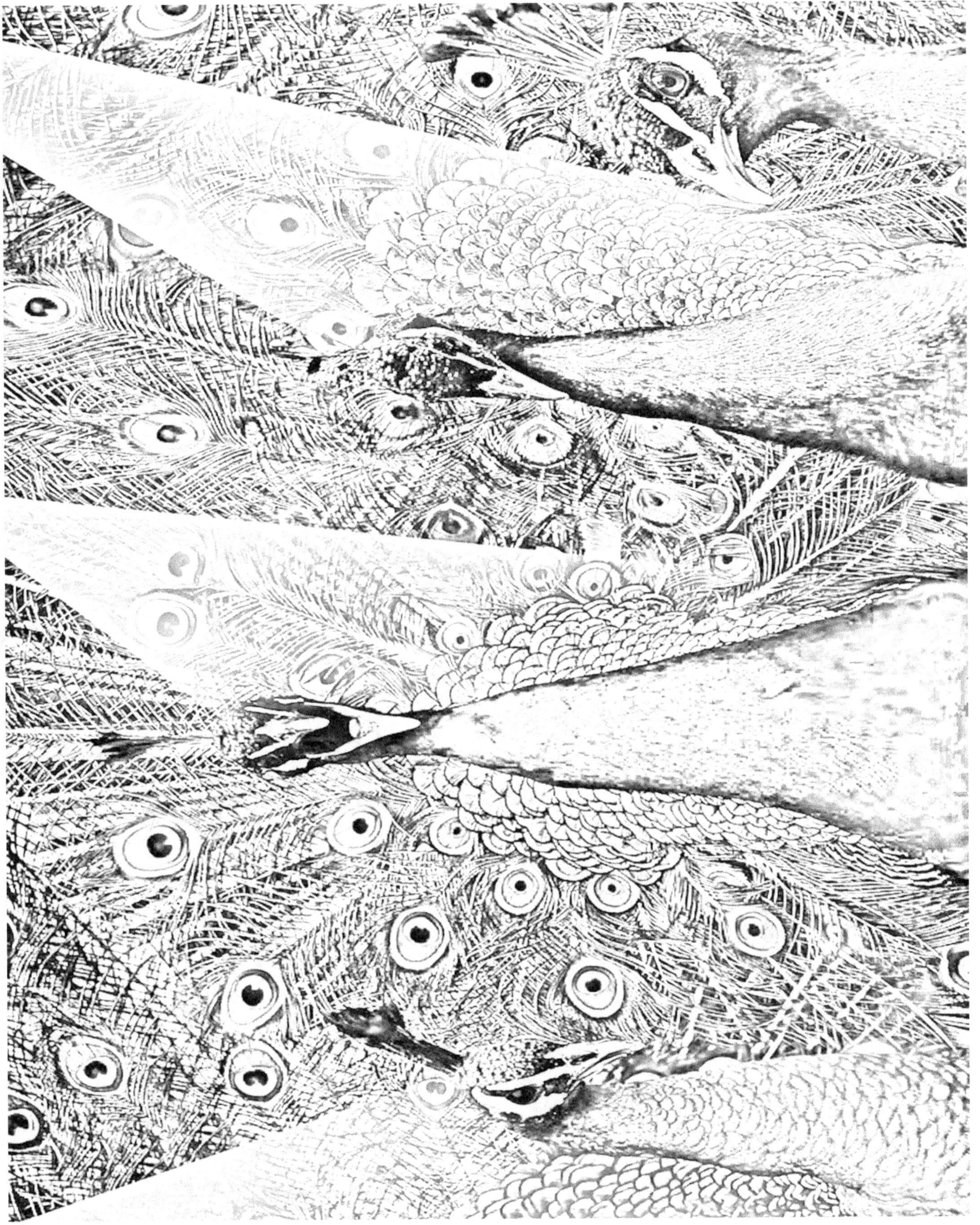

20.   The Butterfly Family

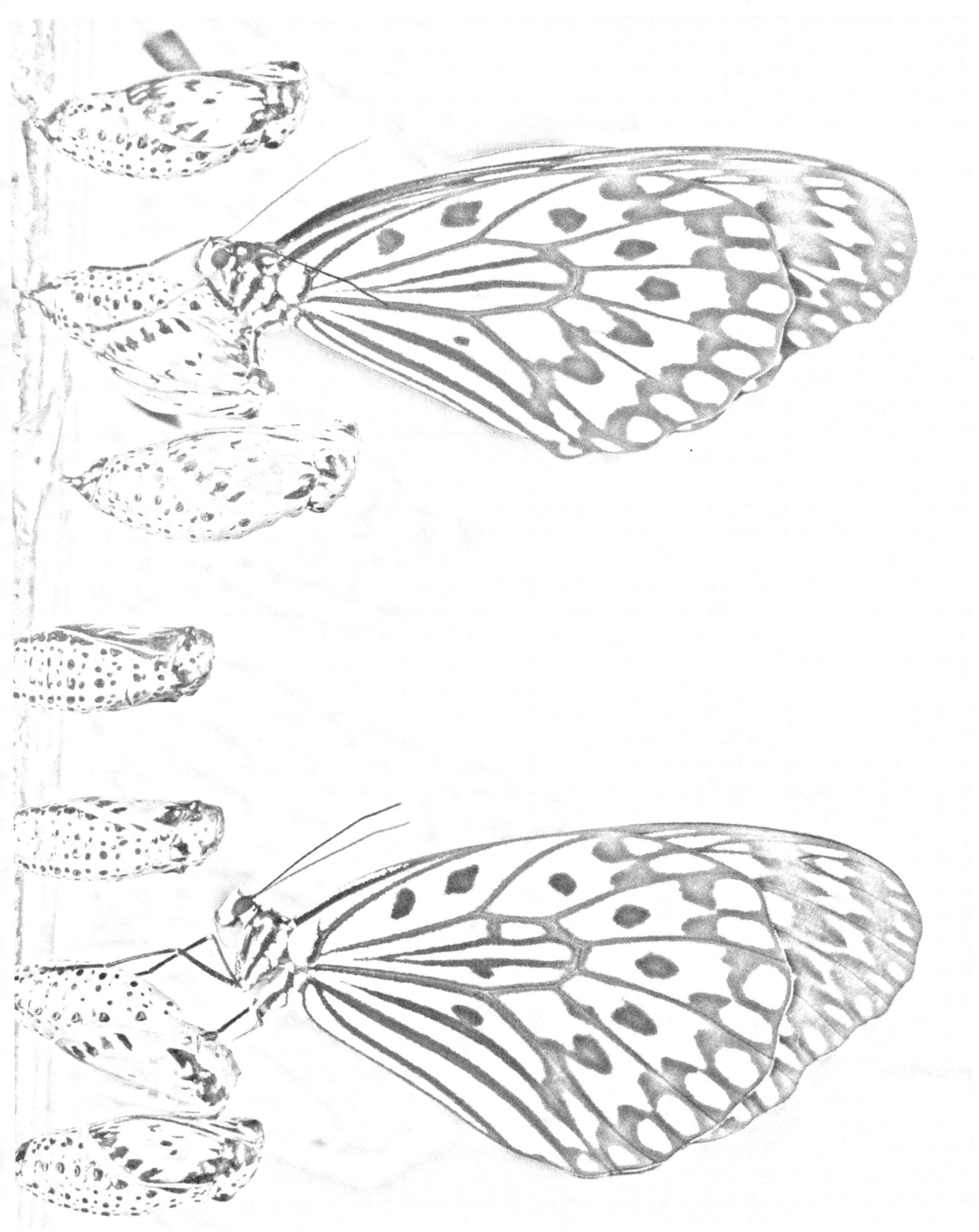